GW00402334

THE DAY OF THE DIPROTODON

First published in 1976 by
Hodder and Stoughton (Australia) Pty Ltd
2 Apollo Place, Lane Cove NSW 2066

© Text Olaf Ruhen, 1976
© Illustrations Peter Pavey, 1976

National Library of Australia Cataloguing-in-Publication Entry

Ruhen, Olaf, 1911–
   The day of the diprotodon

   For children.
   ISBN 0 340 20716 7.

   1. Marsupiala, Fossil—Juvenile literature.
   I. Pavey, Peter, illus.   II. Title.

   599.2

This book is copyright. Apart from any fair dealing
for the purposes of private study, research, criticism
or review, as permitted under the Copyright Act, no part
may be reproduced by any process without written permission.
Inquiries should be addressed to the publishers.

Printed in Hong Kong by Dai Nippon Printing Co (H.K.) Ltd

Reprinted 1977

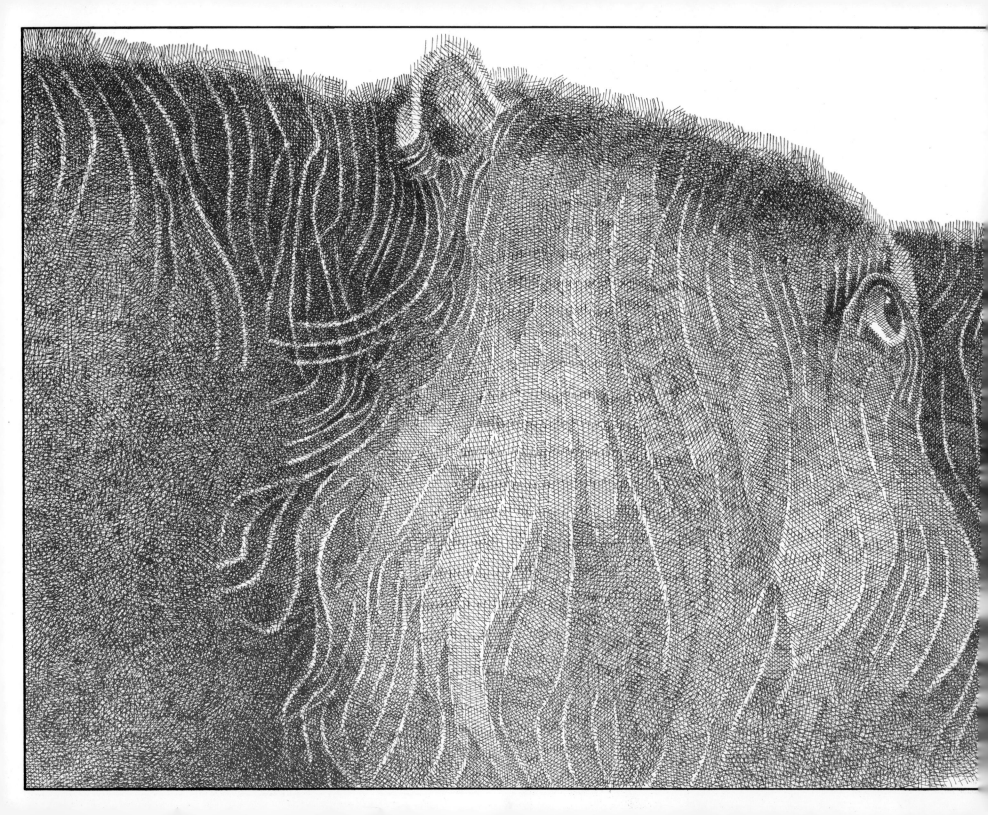

THE DAY OF THE DIPROTODON

Olaf Ruhen   Illustrated by Peter Pavey

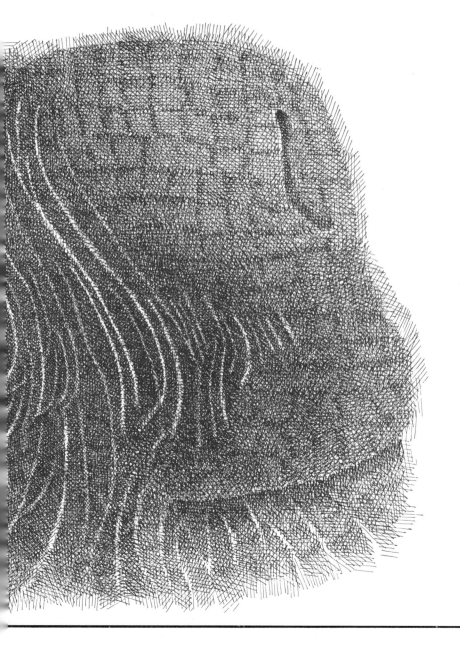

HODDER AND STOUGHTON
SYDNEY AUCKLAND LONDON LEICESTER

The entire dome of the sky was a light steel-blue. There was no wind, nor any significant movement. Only there, where the abundant herbage farther out gave way to the bare, trodden ground surrounding the lake shore, a stray updraft of air now and then stirred up a whorl of dust and was gone, leaving the impression of something cool.

The beasts lay sleepily, grunting uneasily from time to time. They were clustered sparsely beneath the great branching eucalypts that dominated this central plain. Once in a long while, as the climbing sun penetrated the light cover of the branches, one or another rose creakily to its feet to sway into a position farther from the direct rays. Only two or three of the beasts shared the shade of each tree, and only at five or six of the trees within sight were the beasts sheltering.

Beneath other trees scattered among the dry but plentiful shrubs and grasses lay herds of the big plains kangaroo. Some stood as high as two metres, but they still looked small by comparison with the other great beasts. A wedge-tailed eagle hovered high in the sky above, and across the bare stretches of land that set the lake remote from the vegetation, a small group of emu cantered easily, raising dust behind each pulse of their high-stepping claws.

From the lake rim the water had receded; irregular polygons of baked mud stretched far beyond the limits of vision to a point where the heat mirages gave the semblance of a lake, the point at which, indeed, water might still be found.

The parrots, feeding quietly beneath the trees, were silent now. At long intervals the movements of the beasts urged some of them— one or two, a dozen, or a hundred to the safety of the lower branches, and when this happened, as the flock rose the daylight was pierced and split by a dazzling brilliance of plumage, the silence shattered by raucous cries.

The boronia was partly in flower; the heady scent mingled with the acrid smell of the herbivores and the stench of decay that wafted from the dying lake-bed.

The beasts were diprotodons, huge creatures, heavy as the hippopotamus and much the same shape. In them the marsupial kingdom, beginning with the opossums and the phalangers, had risen to its most ambitious height. They had no rivals; they were perhaps the only creatures this land had ever known who had no enemy. Nothing threatened them, nothing worried them. The drifting night shadows did not startle them; the alarms, the antagonisms and the excitements of lesser marsupials or of the birds and reptiles evoked only a mild curiosity from their placid awareness.

Even the young, carried as they were for months beneath the great bulk of their mothers' ponderous bodies, were invulnerable. The marsupial wolves were no match for them; the eagles and the monitors could not find them unattended.

The pouch of the diprotodon, where each young one rode, was an elementary one, consisting only of two great ridges of thick, leathery hide that ran longitudinally down the massive belly of the mother, impressed inwards, so that in the early stages one of the close-folded ridges carried the trivial weight of the minute cub, which needed no other support than this and the determined grip of its small mouth upon the sustaining nipple.

But even in its earliest days the developing cub was equipped with the transverse thumb that gave evidence of the tree-climbing ancestry of the diprotodon; its four legs, converted in this manner to hands and gripping tightly, maintained it in its underslung position as its weight increased.

As the cub developed, and, except for the intervals of feeding and sleeping, relinquished the nipple, it learned to loosen its hold on one side or the other, to twist and watch the way ahead, and to grasp, without leaving its position, handsful of the lush green foliage to supplement its mother's milk.

From sheer aversion to change the mothers carried the cubs in this way until they reached a disproportionate size—until, indeed, proximity to the rough ground and the broken shafts of the shrubs on which its elders had fed made upside-down travel vastly more uncomfortable for the cub than the independence of its own four legs.

In after life it had little use for the inherited tree-climbing hands. No tree that was scaleable could have carried the weight of a diprotodon; nor, once its bulk was acquired, could the creature have maintained itself in tree-climbing attitudes. The young sometimes took a brief interest in their ancestral domain and would climb a little way; but even they were afraid to leave the safety of the central trunk for the branches that bore edible leaves.

The sole remaining use for the gripping hands was in the practice and play of the beasts when they lay on their backs in lush places and rolled from side to side, gripping and bunching all the growing plants within reach and conveying them to their great grinding jaws from four directions at once.

For this reason it was always easy to see where diprotodons had been feeding. There were great cleared wallows where vegetation had been destroyed as well as eaten, where all the lesser trees and shrubs were snapped and broken, and the ground pounded flat. Evidence of a community rich in necessities, a community that had never known scarcity and was careless of its great bounty. In that country such wallows were a commonplace. The sites regenerated themselves quickly, and the areas of destruction were never really widespread, because the diprotodons did not move in herds but in family units.

Nor was there any need for concealment. The abundance of food and the absence of enemies had made it unnecessary for the young to learn to fight; and within the race there was no rivalry. A curious system had evolved in which the young female, when it abandoned its dam, entered upon a brief period of solitary existence, while the young male stayed with the family unit. The male's relationship with the family was broken when he met an acceptable solitary female; so a new unit was established and life quietly continued.

At no season were there proprietary fights amongst the males. Mating was for the duration of life; an old diprotodon left alone by the death of its mate went on eating and sleeping and lying in the sun.

The slow, ponderous movements of the beasts seemed to give them mass even beyond that which they possessed. Their fastest gait was a slow walk, feet bunching as they were lifted and spreading as they were set down, seeming to ensure a safe hold on the earth.

Their legs were short, the feet themselves in-turned, so that a forward movement, though slow, presented an impression of great determination and inevitability. When they were travelling with intent, as they did between watering-place and feeding-ground, at night and in the morning, they covered perhaps four kilometres an hour.

In mid-afternoon the plain came to life. One by one, here and there, the beasts rose unwillingly to their feet and began to graze, slicing the dry yet thick herbage close to the earth, gouging away masses of it, clearing the land like huge, effective, yet unmethodical machines. And as they rose and continued to rise and move about, they dominated the plain.

From hidden patches of sunshine they lurched into view until the whole great salver of the plain took on the appearance of an anthill in slow motion. They grazed aimlessly, from one clump of grasses to another, here pausing to rub their wrinkled hides against a tree; there, standing awkwardly upon three legs, pulling a shrub down to head-level to strip it of its leaves and small branches.

With the approach of sundown the movement changed, became purposeful; from all quarters the beasts converged on the lake, long lines of them traversing the bare wasteland by well-worn tracks; all ardent now for the life-giving waters.

Near the lead, a huge bull diprotodon, two tonnes of inertia, moved complainingly in the heat. Behind him, at about nine metres' distance, his mate followed, her bulk ungainlier even than his because of the well-developed cub that clung to her low-set belly like a strange growth. She grunted and strained, urging herself to keep up with the bull.

The sun was low now, and the blue hills that lined the horizon at an immense distance from the lake were turning to rose and purple in the afternoon light; but the heat shimmer still quivered upwards from the stony ground near the lake shore.

When they reached the well-marked depression that had been the lake edge the bull halted, and, of long custom, swung his head.

Here were still the dead, dull-coloured remnants of the lush sedges; and here, in the days before the long drought, in the previous season when the lake had still lapped its ancient bounds, the bull used to sink his great body in the water, browsing happily on the abundant growth of water-weeds. The water was gone now. It lay eight kilometres away towards the centre of the lake and there were no water-weeds at its verges. It had grown smaller each day with ever-increasing momentum; smaller, and more distant from the creatures' feeding-ground.

The bull stood only a moment, then lowered his head and scrambled down the bank, slipping and sliding through the gravelly dust. More purposefully than before he went ponderously on his way.

The sun had set three hours ago when they reached the water; the moon was high. From east, west and south the long lines of beasts converged, jostling and thrusting in the last accumulation at their goal. Over the last part of the way they seemed to hurry, beckoned by the imminence of their plunge into the lake . . . once hundreds of kilometres in size, now shrunk to the dimensions of a large pool.

Even so, its boundaries were not definite. The last kilometre was a nightmare of sticky, treacherous mud. The bull sank and plunged, reversed his footing and plunged again, sprawling and straining until the mud became smoother and swirled back to fill the tracks he made; then became liquid . . . finally was muddy water. He dipped his snout into it, but did not drink. Head down, he pushed farther into the lake, nosing and tasting the water, thrusting himself between other bodies as big as his own, squeezing past them, and coming eventually to one of the underwater outlets for the springs that flowed upward from the lake-bed and kept the supply replenished. Here the water was fresher, and here the bull drank.

He stayed by the spring a long time, immersed to the shoulders in the water, drinking, lifting his head again to wait, shifting his feet about as they sank into the mud. Once or twice he turned his neck, examining the beasts about him, looking for his mate. After an hour or so he headed back the way he had come, pushing through the great pack of beasts which in happier days had been dispersed along the great shoreline of the waters and now were all brought to this one remaining pool.

The bull was nervous of their presence and their numbers. He disliked the crowd; did he sense dimly, perhaps, that they were responsible for the desperate condition of the muddy water? Near the edge he felt with his feet the body of a young calf, trampled into the grip of the mud; he reared away from it, causing a small local commotion. The water and the thin slurry at its edge were massed with the living, patient bodies of his kind.

He found his mate lying on the outskirts of the press on the more solid mud. She had not slaked her thirst and was moaning with her desire for water. The bull nuzzled her impatiently, and the cub, standing amongst her feet as she lay on her side, did the same. Protestingly she rose, and with the cub by her side she moved towards the press of bodies; but when she came to the thick of them, at the point where the bull had pressed through, she retired, fearful for the young one. She came back to the bull, and waited. At dawn they were still there.

Now the bull was nervous and afraid. By this time, he knew, they should have been back at their feeding-ground, filling their insistent stomachs before the sun's heat made midday sleep imperative. The rhythm of their lives was broken. The bull was afraid, but the cow would not go to the water. As the sun rose, he left her.

There were others heading for the feeding-grounds, but they were moving against a tide, for more beasts were still coming or returning to the pool. With each head-on encounter the bull grew more uneasy, and rocked from side to side before he passed on. In some vague way he knew that the number of his kind using the pool had trebled, had quadrupled overnight, and he was worried, for he was accustomed to a drinking-place he regarded as his own. He could not know that not only had the number who always used the lake been concentrated together, but that hundreds of others had changed their habits to converge on this water because of the drying-up of the creeks, the springs and the billabongs that once dotted the wide plains.

He stood and swayed and rolled his head at each fresh encounter, and the sun was high when at last he staggered into the rich grasslands.

And in the same way as another kilometre or two had separated the waters from the shore in the accelerating effect of the drought, so the great herds of these beasts, converging on the water and cropping and trampling the grasses as they came, had increased the distance from the old shore-line to the feeding-grounds.

When he had slept out his time, the bull stood, hungry and weak because he had missed the morning's feed. Beasts were already on the move towards the water, walking a little, resting briefly, but lying down hardly at all. They were strange new beasts that he did not recognize, of his own kind but from the hinterland, gaunt from thirst and their forced trek. The bull felt resentment rise in him. Dimly he sensed that he should drive them away from his territory, but he had no knowledge of fighting, nor any conception of his latent power.

When one of these beasts came blundering through the wallow where he stood—a young bull followed by an even younger cow, thin, ungainly and without a cub—the anger in the old bull's mind crystallized, and he prepared himself to drive out the intruder. He walked up to him and stood, head to head. Obediently the young bull turned aside. The larger beast put his shoulder against the other's, and used his weight, and again the young bull gave way. But he walked only a step aside and stood his ground.

Thus the old bull tried to teach himself to fight. He used his great clawed hand and later his teeth; but these weapons met only with an unresisting passivity from his opponent. He did not know any technique. He had no knowledge of the anatomy of vulnerability. He did not know that he could tap the life of the youngster at the throat, throttling or biting. He did not know how to paralyze the haunch, slash the belly, lame the leg, blind the eye, crush the skull. He just stood, and pushed, and opened an envious mouth towards the great unassailable escarpment of the upper ribs, the muscle-armoured shoulder of the intruder upon his feeding-ground.

The engagement, such as it was, lasted half an hour. Not even the wedge-tailed eagle, hovering high, gave it a moment's notice. There would be no profit for him from such an encounter, he knew. And then the great bull turned, and, leaving the feed behind him, set out for the lake shore and the water. After an undecided moment his intended victim followed him, puzzled, unhappy.

The lake had not shrunk farther, having reached a size at which its puny springs could keep it replenished; but its verges were crammed now with the bodies of the dead and the dying. The air was heavy with the smell of death: not the sweet, slavering scent of slaughter, but the thick, repulsive stench of ultimate exhaustion, the heavy breath of starvation, the gases of corruption. A huge monitor lizard, eight metres long, was gorging on the carcasses, keeping a watchful yet contemptuous eye on the living beasts.

The bull pushed and struggled, side-stepping, tasting the mud until he came to the fresher water from the springs; then he drank deep. Immediately the cramps seized his belly and he gave vent to the soft, muted complaint of his kind; an inadequate moaning, like the love-song of a rhinoceros. Hastily, lifting his feet, slipping and sliding in panic, he returned to the denser mud at the verges. And lay there.

After a time the pains eased; he struggled to his feet and went to find his mate. She was not far away, almost at the same place he had left her the previous night; but the cub was gone. It was nowhere to be seen. He called to the cow and she moved her great bulk once or twice as though she were trying to get to her feet, but she could not rise. Moaning, the bull stood over her through the night.

The sun rose bright again, for the two hundred and seventieth day of drought. The beasts could not know that this was the first definitive sign of the recession of the Ice Age, whose approach, some few thousand years before, had transformed these sub-tropical plains into a temperate paradise. Nor could they know that never again would the lake hold water, except for that tiny pool: all that was left, now, near the central mound spring. They knew only that the sun was climbing high and that their rhythm was disturbed; that now they were at the water when they should have been at the feeding-place. Some few were travelling, some coming, some going. The rest lay entangled, though not trapped, in the sticky mud.

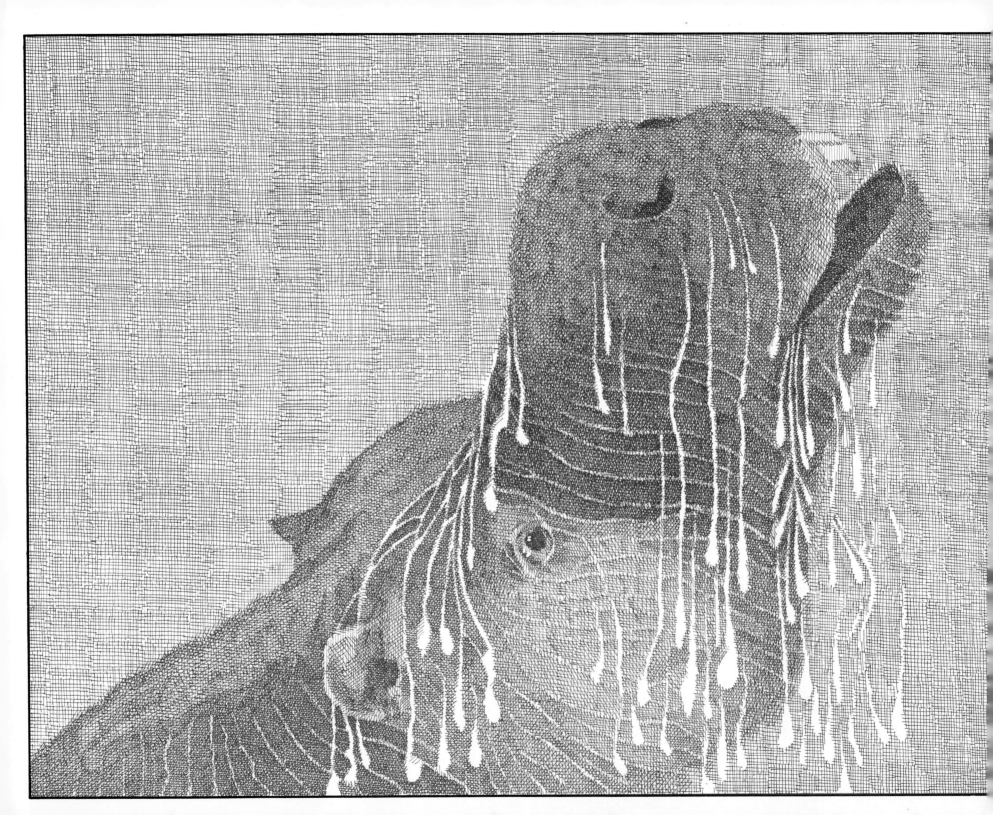

When the sun rose high, the bull tried to prod the cow to her feet, but she would not, or could not rise. He stirred himself and went towards the water. When he had advanced sufficiently for it to be liquid enough, he lowered himself into it until only his head was above the surface . . . as he had so often lain at the lakeside in happier days. It was cooler there and he felt more contented, though even now the pangs of hunger were beginning to give place to the more muted and less urgent agonies of starvation.

In mid-afternoon he came out of the pool and made his way back to where his mate was lying. She was dead. He nuzzled the body for a long time, standing with his head against her great side, his small eyes blinking; a tragi-comic figure, bloated, mud-covered, puzzled, hungry and sorrowing. Pathetic in his tragedy, yet lacking nobility of stature. About him the mud-covered bodies lay sprawled and humped, hundreds on hundreds of them. Here and there was movement, a slavering head rolling, a survivor picking his way, the chattering of flocks of small birds, and the watchful eyes, the flickering tongues of the big lizards.

But such life only served to emphasize the desolation of death. A dripping body lunged upward from the deeper part of the pool and stood, hesitating, looking for a path amongst the carcasses. The young and the old, bulls and cows and cubs lay all together.

With night approaching, the bull turned to the long trail that led to the feeding-grounds. He picked his way amongst the silent, mud-covered mounds. The bodies lined the track, too, not thickly as they lined the pool, but with sufficient frequency to make it a road of horror. But the bull felt no horror, only hunger, exhaustion and a vague anger.

A kilometre from the watering-place he met yet another of his kind, gaunt from long travel, hobbling painfully towards the pool through the dry dust of the lake bed. Neither gave way. Heads lowered, they advanced until their noses were touching, then stood still. Then the bull laid into the other's shoulders and pushed, and the stranger strained against him. Ludicrously their heads slid apart; their necks twisted and they fell, each past the other; they flopped in the dust.

Too late, within the bull's small brain was born the desire to kill; a desire come too late for him to protect his domain and his family; and in his adversary, it was come too late to win him to the waters and the life they promised. Only the watchful vigilance of a creature beset throughout a lifetime by his enemies could have brought either through a disaster such as this. Only the lessons of an aggressive infancy could have armed him; only vigilance and the practice developed in a hundred fights could have urged and sustained the one or the other to victory. And here they were, senescent at the end of a long road, applying themselves to a youngster's lessons.

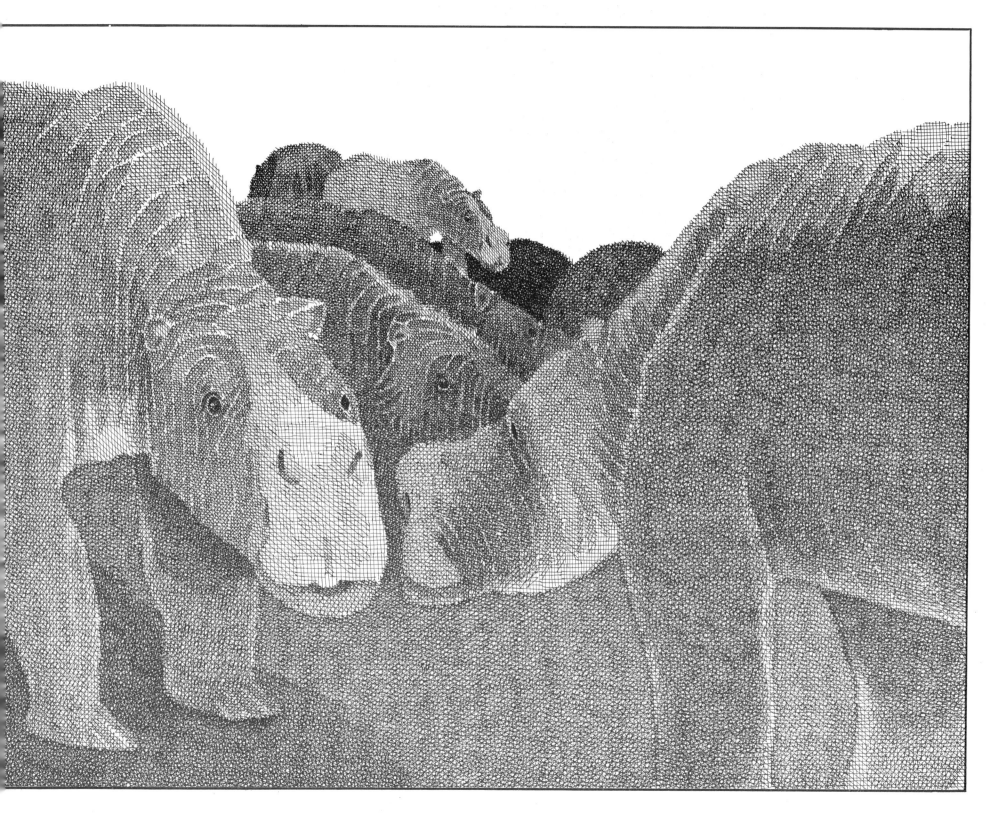

From the ground the bull swung his forequarters and bit viciously at the hind foot of the stranger, grabbing at the short, heavy cannon-bone with his forefoot as though it were the trunk of a young tree. The stranger kicked him on the nose, harmlessly, evading the over-slow clutch and bite almost by accident. They dragged themselves to their feet, and stood looking at each other, their little eyes red-rimmed, their purposes great and their methods undiscovered. Again and again they came to an encounter, again and again unavailingly. And there they died, not from injury but from frustration, obstinacy and the sheer excesses of exhaustion.

They are still there, two faint humps on the cracked dry bed of Lake Callabonna in the State of South Australia, a kilometre from the mound springs in the centre of the lake. For that day, or the day that followed . . . or perhaps the day after that was the last day of the diprotodon, the day the species vanished from the earth in that place. Fifty thousand years is not, after all, so long a day upon the calendar of time. The mud has preserved them where they fell, the mud and the hot sun, and today their attitudes still attest the frustration of their intentions.

But the vulnerable ones, the kangaroo, the monitor lizard, the parrot and the wedge-tailed eagle, still crowd the sunny plains.

A NOTE ON THE DIPROTODON

The diprotodon was a creature of the Pleistocene period, which ended about fifty thousand years ago. A gigantic pouched mammal, herbivorous, it is linked to the present-day kangaroo, wallaby and wombat of Australia.

The first scientific expedition to Lake Callabonna, an area of eight hectares situated in the north-east of South Australia, took place in 1893 and was led by Henry Hurst of the South Australian Museum. The Hurst expedition reported: " The diprotodon skeletons were found distributed about in all directions, most of them partly exposed on the surface and lying in the positions in which they had died. The remains of more than two hundred diprotodons can be counted within a radius of half a mile from the camp."

In 1953, Professor A A Stirton, of the University of California, led a second expedition, financed by the Fulbright Awards, the South Australian Museum and the University of California, to the area. This time it was estimated that as many as a thousand massive diprotodon skeletons in perfect condition might lie beneath the sticky saline clay. Professor Stirton reported: " Never have I seen the evidence of so many complete skeletons of gigantic extinct animals in such a small area."

Although the drought that dried Lake Callabonna brought death to such a large number of these prehistoric creatures, the diprotodon did not become extinct until many centuries later. They existed in areas throughout Australia; the first skeleton to be discovered in modern times was found in 1830 by a member of Sir Thomas Mitchell's expedition, at the Wellington Caves of New South Wales.